The Best of
FAVORITE RECIPES FROM QUILTERS

SALADS

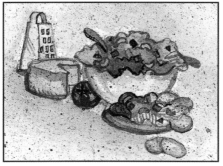

Louise Stoltzfus

Good Books
Intercourse, PA 17534
Printed and bound in Hong Kong

Cover design and illustrations by Cheryl Benner
Design by Dawn J. Ranck

SALADS: THE BEST OF FAVORITE RECIPES FROM
QUILTERS

Copyright © 1994 by Good Books, Intercourse, Pennsylvania
17534
International Standard Book Number: 1-56148-113-0
Library of Congress Catalog Card Number: 94-14903

Library of Congress Cataloging-in-Publication Data

Breads / [compiled by] Louise Stoltzfus.
        p. cm. — (The Best of Favorite recipes from quilters)
     Includes index.
     ISBN 1-56148-111-4 : $7.95
     1. Salad. I. Stoltzfus, Louise, 1952- . II. Series.
TX740.S275   1994
641.8'3—dc20
                                                        94-14903
                                                         CIP

INTRODUCTION

Amid the rush and haste of life, many people seek rest and quiet in community life. Quilters find community in common goals and activities. They talk of needles and thread, fabric and stitches, and bedcovers and pieces of art. They gather in homes, fabric shops, and convention centers to share their ideas and projects.

Many quilters are also homemakers. Some treat both cooking and quilting as high art forms. Others work hard to prepare varied and healthful meals for their busy families and quilt when they have free time.

From Shrimp and Crab Salad to Hungarian Cucumber Salad to Grape Salad, these Salad recipes are both practical and delicious. Those who love to quilt and those who love to cook will share in the special vibrancy of this small collection.

A FAVORITE LUNCHEON TURKEY SALAD

Connee Sager, Tucson, AZ

2½-3 lb. turkey
20-oz. can water chestnuts
2 lbs. seedless grapes
2 cups sliced celery
2-3 cups toasted, slivered almonds
3 cups mayonnaise
1 Tbsp. curry powder
2 Tbsp. soy sauce
2 Tbsp. lemon juice (optional)
Lettuce
20-oz. can pineapple chunks, drained
Fresh mint leaves (optional)

1. Cook, cool and bone turkey. Cut into bite-sized pieces. Drain and slice water chestnuts. Remove grapes from stems.
2. Combine turkey, water chestnuts, grapes, celery and 1½-2 cups toasted almonds.
3. In a separate bowl mix mayonnaise, curry powder, soy sauce and lemon juice. Combine with turkey mixture. Chill for several hours or overnight.
4. Spoon onto a bed of lettuce arranged on individual serving plates. Sprinkle with remaining almonds and garnish with pineapple chunks and mint leaves.

Makes 12 or more servings

BEEF AND LENTIL SALAD

Jay Conrad, Bedford, TX

1½ quarts water
1 tsp. salt
1 cup lentils
½ lb. roast beef
3 large bell peppers, sliced
3 scallions with tops, sliced
½ cup chopped fresh parsley
¼ cup chopped fresh dill
1 clove garlic, minced
2 Tbsp. olive oil
2 Tbsp. vinegar
1 tsp. Dijon mustard
Salt and pepper to taste
8 lettuce leaves
1-2 tomatoes
8 sprigs parsley
8 sprigs dill

1. Heat water and 1 tsp. salt in large saucepan to boiling. Add lentils, reduce heat and simmer until lentils are just tender, but not soft. Drain and cool.
2. Cut roast beef into narrow 2-inch strips.
3. Combine lentils, beef, peppers, scallions, chopped parsley and chopped dill in large bowl.
4. Whisk garlic, oil, vinegar and mustard together. Add to lentil and beef mixture and season to taste with salt and pepper. Refrigerate to chill.
5. Serve on lettuce leaves and garnish with tomato slices, parsley sprigs and dill sprigs. Accompany with rolls or muffins.

Makes 8 servings

My friend Lenay and I are each mothers of two small children. We try to make time to quilt together at least one night a week. While we quilt, we also unwind, share our problems and sip tea often until long after midnight.

Bea Gagliano, Lakewood, NJ

TURKEY SALAD

Jean Swift, Comfrey, MN

1 cup elbow macaroni
2 cups cooked turkey
1 cup diced celery
11-oz. can mandarin oranges, drained
⅓ cup slivered almonds
1 cup grapes
1 cup mayonnaise
Pinch salt
¾ cup whipping cream

1. Cook macaroni according to directions. Drain, rinse and cool.
2. Combine all ingredients except cream. Refrigerate overnight.
3. Whip cream. Stir into salad and serve.

Makes 10-15 servings

Since I've gotten into quilting, my cooking and baking have fallen off drastically! Every quilter needs someone to cook for him or her.

Jay Conrad, Bedford, TX

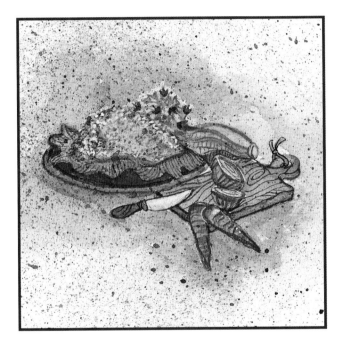

TUNA SPINACH SALAD

Susan L. Schwarz, North Bethesda, MD

Salad
6-8 slices bacon
1 lb. fresh spinach
1 cup water chestnuts, sliced
1 cup bean sprouts
3-4 hard-boiled eggs, sliced
7-oz. can tuna, drained and flaked

Dressing
½ cup sugar or less
¼ cup vinegar
1 cup cooking oil
⅓ cup ketchup
1 Tbsp. Worcestershire sauce
1 medium onion, finely chopped

1. Fry, drain and crumble bacon. Combine all salad ingredients and refrigerate.
2. To prepare dressing combine sugar and vinegar in small saucepan over low heat until sugar dissolves. Remove from heat, combine all ingredients and shake well. Refrigerate until serving time.
3. Immediately before serving, combine dressing with salad and toss well.

Makes 6-8 servings

SHRIMP AND CRAB SALAD

Charmaine Keith, Marion, KS

4 cups cooked pasta
3 hard-boiled eggs, sliced
1-1½ cups small shrimp
1-1½ cups crab meat
8-oz. can black olives, diced
1 small onion, diced
3-4 stalks celery, diced
Salt to taste
Cajun seasoning to taste
1 cup mayonnaise

1. Combine pasta, eggs, shrimp and crab and refrigerate until cold.
2. In large bowl mix all ingredients, adding enough mayonnaise to hold salad together nicely.
3. Serve with garlic bread.

Note: *Do not use canned shrimp as it will not flavor salad. Use small fresh shrimp, steamed in boiling water until pink and until white color has appeared, about 3 to 5 minutes. Imitation crab meat will work very nicely. If your Cajun seasoning has salt in it, do not add extra salt.*

Makes 12 or more servings

Seafood Pasta Salad

Susan Orleman, Pittsburgh, PA

16-oz. pkg. pasta
1 lb. fresh shrimp
½ lb. crab meat
1 cup frozen peas
3 green onions, chopped
3 medium tomatoes, chopped
¾ cup olive oil
¼ cup chopped fresh parsley
⅓ cup wine vinegar
1 tsp. dried oregano
1½ tsp. dried basil
½ tsp. garlic salt
½ tsp. coarsely ground pepper

1. Cook pasta according to package directions, omitting salt. Drain and rinse with cold water.
2. Steam and peel shrimp.
3. Combine all ingredients and toss gently. Chill and serve.

Makes 10 servings

PAT'S PASTA SALAD

Barbara A. Nolan, Pleasant Valley, NY

1 lb. small pasta
2 Tbsp. flour
¾ cup sugar
1 tsp. salt
2 eggs
2 15-oz. cans pineapple chunks
2 11-oz. cans mandarin oranges, drained
2 9-oz. cartons whipped topping
1 medium jar maraschino cherries

1. Cook pasta 6-8 minutes in boiling water. Do not overcook. Drain and rinse with cold water.
2. In a saucepan combine flour, sugar and salt. Add eggs and juice from pineapple. Cook until thickened. Cool.
3. Mix cooled sauce, pineapple chunks and oranges with pasta. Refrigerate overnight.
4. Fold whipped topping and cherries into pasta salad and mix thoroughly.
5. Garnish with fruit of choice.

Note: *This may be very watery at first, but it will firm up as it stands. May be made several days ahead of time.*

Makes 20 servings

SPAGHETTI SALAD

Barbara Wenders, Moscow, ID

Salad
7-oz. pkg. angel hair spaghetti
1 green pepper
1 red pepper
1-2 green onions
1 large tomato
1 zucchini
3 stalks celery
¼ cup Parmesan cheese

Dressing
¼ cup red wine vinegar
¼ cup olive oil
2 Tbsp. dry Italian dressing mix
1 Tbsp. parsley
1 Tbsp. sugar

1. To prepare salad cook angel hair, rinse and cool. Dice vegetables.
2. To prepare dressing combine all ingredients and chill.
3. Toss pasta with vegetables. Sprinkle with dressing and toss again. Add Parmesan cheese and chill overnight.

Makes 12 servings

CURRIED RICE SALAD

Gwen Oberg, Albuquerque, NM

½ cup uncooked rice
1 Tbsp. vinegar
2 Tbsp. cooking oil
¾ cup mayonnaise
1 tsp. salt or less
¾ tsp. curry powder
¼ cup chopped onion
1 cup chopped celery
10-oz. pkg. frozen peas

1. Cook rice according to directions.
2. Meanwhile, combine vinegar, cooking oil, mayonnaise, salt and curry powder. Add cooked rice to this mixture and stir in onion while rice is still hot. Chill.
3. Fold in celery and peas and serve.

Makes 6-8 servings

POTATO AND EGG SALAD

Diana Huntress Deem, Bethesda, MD

6-8 medium red potatoes
3 hard-boiled eggs
2 medium dill pickles
1 cup mayonnaise
1 tsp. dry mustard

1. Cook potatoes in water to cover. Cool and dice.
2. Chop eggs and pickles into very small pieces.
   Combine with potatoes in serving bowl.
3. Thoroughly mix mayonnaise and mustard. Stir into
   potato salad and mix well. Chill until ready to serve.

Makes 8-10 servings

Childhood memories of food and quilts have always gone together for me. My grandmother had a beautiful quilt bordered in green with white panels of red and pink tulips which she used as a picnic tablecloth. We would lay the quilt on a grassy hill and arrange our bounty of fried chicken, potato salad and lemon iced tea on it, enjoying the ever-blooming flowers on our table year-round.

Barbara Sparks, Glen Burnie, MD

POTATO SALAD

Alma Mullet, Walnut Creek, OH

Salad
6 boiled potatoes, diced
2 small onions, diced
3 hard-boiled eggs, diced
1 stalk celery, finely chopped
1 small sweet pickle, finely chopped

Dressing
2 Tbsp. flour
½ cup vinegar
3 Tbsp. prepared mustard
3 Tbsp. sugar
2 tsp. salt
3 eggs, separated
1 cup sour cream
Seasoning to taste

1. Combine all salad ingredients. Set aside.
2. To prepare dressing combine all ingredients except egg whites and sour cream in a saucepan. Bring to a boil, stirring constantly until thickened. Cool mixture.
3. Beat egg whites and sour cream together. Fold into dressing mixture. Season to taste.
4. Pour cooled dressing over salad and serve.

Makes 6-8 servings

MEXICAN SALAD

Betty L. Richards, Rapid City, SD
Patti Boston, Coshocton, OH
Judy Berry, Columbia, MD

1 head lettuce, shredded
2 tomatoes, chopped
1 medium onion, chopped
1 lb. cheddar cheese, shredded
16-oz. can pinto or kidney beans, drained
12-oz. bottle Catalina dressing
15-oz. pkg. corn or taco chips

1. Toss lettuce, tomatoes and onion in large bowl. Add cheese and beans.
2. Immediately before serving, toss with dressing.
3. Serve with chips.

Makes 10-12 servings

TACO SALAD

MaryJane S. Pozarycki, Neptune City, NJ

1 head lettuce, shredded
2-3 tomatoes, cut in wedges
1 cucumber, thinly sliced
½-1 cup chopped onion
8-oz. bottle Italian salad dressing
1 lb. ground beef
1 pkg. dry taco seasoning
8 ozs. cheddar cheese, grated
6-oz. pkg. taco chips, crumbled

1. In a large bowl combine lettuce, tomatoes, cucumber, onion and salad dressing.
2. Brown ground beef. Drain excess fat. Stir in taco seasoning and cool.
3. Fold ground beef and cheese into salad. Immediately before serving, add taco chips and mix well.

Makes 6-8 servings

Variation: *Add 16-oz. can chickpeas, drained, to salad along with cheese.*

Jacquelyn Kreitzer, Mechanicsburg, PA

SEVEN-LAYER SALAD

Lori Drohman, Rogue River, OR
Esther S. Martin, Ephrata, PA

Salad
1 head lettuce
1 cup chopped celery
4 hard-boiled eggs, sliced
10-oz. pkg. frozen peas
½ green pepper, sliced
1 medium onion, sliced
1 cup grated carrots
3-oz. jar bacon bits

Dressing
2 cups mayonnaise
2 Tbsp. sugar
4 ozs. cheddar cheese, grated

1. Tear lettuce and arrange in 9" x 13" pan. Layer remaining salad ingredients in the order listed.
2. To prepare dressing combine mayonnaise and sugar and spread over salad. Top with grated cheddar cheese.
3. Refrigerate 8-10 hours before serving.

Makes 8 servings

GREEK PEASANT SALAD

Joan T. Schneider, Seaford, NY

Salad

1 large head romaine lettuce
2 medium tomatoes, cut in wedges
1 large cucumber, sliced
6-8 radishes, thinly sliced
4-6 green onions, sliced
6 ozs. feta cheese, coarsely crumbled
¼ lb. Greek black olives
1 tsp. minced fresh mint (optional)

Dressing

3 Tbsp. lemon juice
2 Tbsp. red wine vinegar
1 clove garlic, crushed
½ tsp. minced fresh oregano

1. Wash, drain and chill lettuce. Tear into large bowl. Add vegetables, cheese and olives. Sprinkle with mint.
2. Blend all dressing ingredients in small bowl with whisk. Pour over salad and toss lightly. Serve immediately.

Makes 6-8 servings

THREE-BEAN SALAD

Barbara F. Shie, Colorado Springs, CO

Salad
16-oz. can string beans, drained
16-oz. can wax beans, drained
16-oz. can kidney beans, drained
4-oz. can diced pimentos
2 small onions, diced
1 green pepper, diced

Dressing
⅓ cup cooking oil
⅔ cup vinegar
⅔ cup sugar
½ tsp. pepper
1 tsp. salt or less
2 tsp. celery seeds

1. Combine all salad ingredients and set aside.
2. Combine all dressing ingredients and pour over salad. Toss well and refrigerate in covered container. Better if prepared several days in advance.

Variation: *I add a 16-oz. can black-eyed peas and call this Four-Bean Salad. I also substitute the following dressing:* ½ *cup sugar,* ½ *cup vinegar,* ½ *cup cooking oil, 2 Tbsp. snipped parsley,* ½ *tsp. dried basil and* ½ *tsp. salt.*

Shirley Norris, Walhonding, OH

Makes 6-8 servings

My mother grew up in Missouri among avid quilters, and all of her family quilts were very traditional. When she and my father retired, they moved to Tucson, Arizona. During the time of their 40th wedding anniversary, they planned a trip to West Virginia to visit my family. While I had not yet completed a full-size quilt, I decided to make them a Moon Over Mountain quilt—a Southwest pattern and very different from the other quilts in our family.

At the party Mom opened the package and just sat there. (She didn't know I had started to quilt.) Finding it hard to believe that I had made the quilt and with tears streaming down her face, she asked, "How did you know how?"

Carol Weaver, Houston, TX

PAM'S CAESAR SALAD

Pamela R. Kerschner, Stevensville, MD

Dressing
1 cup olive oil
⅓ cup red wine vinegar
3 Tbsp. fresh lemon juice
2 tsp. salt or less
1½ tsp. freshly ground black pepper
2 cloves garlic, peeled and halved

Salad
3 large heads romaine lettuce
1 lb. mushrooms
16-oz. can pitted, ripe olives
¾ cup grated Parmesan cheese
½ box croutons

1. To prepare dressing measure all ingredients into container with tight-fitting lid. Shake to blend. Refrigerate to chill.
2. Bring dressing to room temperature. Remove garlic pieces and discard.
3. Wash, drain and dry romaine. Tear into large mixing bowl.
4. Wash and dry mushrooms. Slice thinly into lettuce.
5. Drain and slice olives into salad. Sprinkle with Parmesan cheese.
6. Pour dressing over salad and toss well to coat all ingredients. Add croutons, toss and serve immediately.

Makes 12-15 servings

RED CABBAGE SLAW

Virginia Dunkline, Florence, SC

Salad
½ large head red cabbage, grated
4 green onions, chopped
1 pkg. chicken-flavored Ramen noodles
½ cup toasted sliced almonds
2 Tbsp. sesame seed

Dressing
2 Tbsp. sugar
½ cup cooking oil
1 tsp. salt
1 Tbsp. vinegar
½ tsp. pepper
Seasoning pkg. of Ramen noodles

1. Combine all salad ingredients and set aside.
2. Combine all dressing ingredients and mix well. Stir into cabbage mixture immediately before serving.

Variation: *To serve as a main dish add 3 diced, cooked chicken breasts to salad ingredients.*

Doris Morelock, Alexandria, VA

Makes 10-12 servings

SOUTH RIVER CABBAGE SALAD

Marsha Sands, Ocean City, MD

Salad
½ head cabbage, thinly sliced
½ green pepper, thinly sliced
1 carrot, grated
1 celery stalk, chopped
1 apple, chopped
1 Tbsp. finely chopped onion

Dressing
1 cup mayonnaise
1½ Tbsp. Worcestershire sauce
½ tsp. onion salt
2 Tbsp. prepared mustard
2 Tbsp. cider vinegar
½ cup sugar
½ tsp. pepper
½ tsp. celery seed

1. Combine all salad ingredients and set aside.
2. Combine all dressing ingredients and beat until thoroughly mixed. Chill.
3. Immediately before serving, toss dressing with vegetables.

Makes 6 servings

CREAMY COLESLAW

Dottie Geraci, Burtonsville, MD

3-oz. pkg. lemon gelatin
¼ tsp. salt
1 cup boiling water
1 Tbsp. vinegar
½ cup cold water
½ cup mayonnaise
½ cup sour cream
1 tsp. grated onion
1 Tbsp. prepared mustard
3 cups finely shredded cabbage
2 Tbsp. chopped green pepper
1 Tbsp. chopped parsley

1. Dissolve gelatin and salt in boiling water. Add vinegar and cold water and mix well. Stir in all remaining ingredients, blending thoroughly.
2. Pour into mold or serving dish and chill until firm. Serve.

Makes 6-8 servings

FRESH BROCCOLI SALAD

Beatrice Orgish, Richardson, TX

Salad
2 bunches fresh broccoli
10 slices bacon, cooked and crumbled
⅔ cup raisins
¼-½ purple onion, chopped

Dressing
1 cup mayonnaise
⅓ cup sugar
2 Tbsp. red wine vinegar

1. Wash and cut broccoli into bite-sized pieces.
2. Combine broccoli, bacon, raisins and onion in a large bowl.
3. In a separate bowl mix mayonnaise, sugar and vinegar. Pour dressing over salad and toss.
4. Refrigerate at least 2 hours before serving, tossing occasionally.

Variations on Fresh Broccoli Salad:
Substitute ½-¾ cup sliced almonds for onion.

Jean H. Robinson, Cinnaminson, NJ

Add 1 cup frozen peas and 1 cup sunflower seeds.

Laura Heller, Delanco, NJ

Substitute 6 ozs. grated mozzarella cheese for raisins.

Barbara Sparks, Glen Burnie, MD

Omit raisins and substitute bacon bits for bacon.

Rayann Rohrer, Allentown, PA

Makes 8 servings

Our grandson, Brandon, stayed with us two days a week for about three years. He liked to watch me quilt. When he was two, he would stick quilting pins in rows and call that quilting. By the time he was three, he wanted a needle and thread. I did not knot the thread, and he could "sew" for a long time. He wised up to me and asked for a knot in his thread. The last quilt he "helped" me with before going to nursery school was a Cat Quilt for his mother. I left his stitches in the quilt, and, of course, it has become a family conversation piece. One is never too young to learn to quilt!

Violette Denney, Carrollton, GA

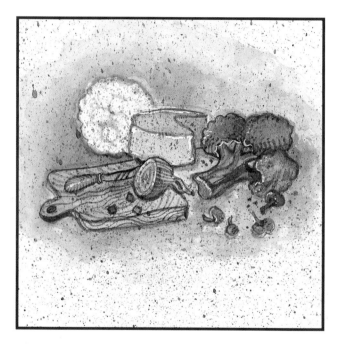

BROCCOLI CAULIFLOWER SALAD

Edna Stoltzfus, Leola, PA

Salad
8-10 slices bacon
1 head broccoli
1 head cauliflower
1 cup grated cheese
1 small onion, diced

Dressing
½ cup sour cream
½ cup mayonnaise
½ cup sugar

1. Fry, drain and crumble bacon.
2. Chop broccoli and cauliflower into large serving dish. Add bacon, cheese and onion and toss.
3. Thoroughly mix all dressing ingredients. Pour over salad and mix well. Serve.

Makes 20 servings

HUNGARIAN CUCUMBER SALAD

Maureen Csikasz, Wakefield, MA

2 cucumbers
1 Tbsp. salt or less
½ cup water
¼ cup vinegar
⅛ cup sugar
Paprika

1. Peel and grate cucumbers. Sprinkle with salt and let stand 1 hour.
2. Squeeze excess juice out of cucumbers. Place cucumbers in serving bowl. Pour water, vinegar and sugar over cucumbers and mix lightly. Chill in refrigerator.
3. Sprinkle with paprika and serve.

Makes 4 servings

CUCUMBER SALAD

Colleen Kern, Oakland, NJ

1 Tbsp. dehydrated onion flakes
¼ tsp. dried parsley
1 tsp. sugar
1 tsp. salt
1 Tbsp. lemon juice
1 tsp. celery seed
¼ cup vinegar
¼ tsp. Accent (optional)
⅛ tsp. pepper
2 cucumbers, peeled and sliced

1. Combine all ingredients in a bowl and stir well.
2. Refrigerate for several hours before serving.

Makes 4 servings

MARINATED CARROT SALAD

Florence Heard, St. Marys, ON

2 lbs. carrots
1 medium onion
1 medium green pepper
½ cup tomato soup
¼ cup sugar
½ cup cooking oil
⅓ cup vinegar
½ tsp. dry mustard
½ tsp. salt
¼ tsp. pepper

1. Peel and cut carrots into ¼-inch diagonal slices. Cook in boiling salted water until just tender, about 6 to 8 minutes. (Do not overcook.) Drain.
2. Slice onion thinly and separate. Seed and cut green pepper into thin strips. Add onion rings and green pepper strips to carrots.
3. In a small jar combine all remaining ingredients. Shake to blend. Pour over vegetables. Marinate at least 12-24 hours in refrigerator.
4. To serve lift vegetables out of dressing and transfer to a serving bowl.

Makes 6-8 servings

GRANDMA BARTEL'S CHEESE SALAD

Cheryl Bartel, Hillsboro, KS

2 20-oz. cans pineapple chunks
3 egg yolks, beaten
½ cup sugar
1 heaping Tbsp. flour
½ lb. Velveeta cheese, cubed
1 small pkg. marshmallows

1. Drain pineapples and reserve juice.
2. In a saucepan combine egg yolks, sugar, flour and pineapple juice. Cook until clear, stirring frequently.
3. Remove from heat and add pineapple chunks, cheese and marshmallows and toss well.

Makes 10 servings

Once a month our quilting group of twelve women meets to work on our own projects and share a potluck lunch. Because we sometimes discuss how much bother it is to prepare a dish, we recently decided to vote on abandoning the potluck. However, everyone voted to continue because we so enjoy eating each other's food.

Carolee Kidd, Albuquerque, NM

CRANBERRY GELATIN SALAD

Marge Jarrett, Gaithersburg, MD

1 lb. fresh cranberries
2 cups ground apples
1½ cups sugar
1 tsp. lemon juice
6-oz. pkg. raspberry gelatin
½ cup chopped walnuts
½ cup chopped celery

1. Grind cranberries and apples separately in food grinder.
2. Combine cranberries, apples, sugar and lemon juice and let stand several hours, stirring occasionally.
3. Prepare gelatin according to package directions. When cooled, but not set, stir in fruit mixture, walnuts and celery.
4. Pour into serving dish and refrigerate until set.

Variation: *Omit apples. Add 1 cup sour cream along with walnuts and celery.*

Julianna Csikasz, Wakefield, MA

SPINACH STRAWBERRY SALAD

Deb Koelsch, Lancaster, PA

Salad
12 ozs. fresh spinach
1 quart strawberries
2 tsp. sesame seed

Dressing
½ cup cooking oil
¼ cup vinegar
¼ tsp. Worcestershire sauce
½ cup sugar
¼ tsp. paprika
1½ tsp. grated onion

1. Wash and drain spinach. Tear bite-sized pieces into serving bowl. Add strawberries and sesame seed and toss.
2. To prepare dressing blend together all ingredients.
3. Toss dressing with salad and serve immediately.

Makes 6 servings

CRANBERRY HOLIDAY SALAD

Shirley Norris, Walhonding, OH

6-oz. pkg. raspberry gelatin
1 cup boiling water
16-oz. can whole berry cranberry sauce
20-oz. can crushed pineapple, drained
½ cup chopped walnuts
8-oz. pkg. cream cheese, softened
1 cup sour cream
¼ cup chopped walnuts

1. Combine gelatin and boiling water in a large bowl. Stir in cranberry sauce and break up into gelatin mixture. Add pineapple and ½ cup walnuts and mix well. Pour into 9" x 13" pan. Refrigerate until set.
2. Beat together cream cheese and sour cream and spread over salad. Sprinkle with ¼ cup walnuts and serve.

Makes 12 servings

CRANBERRY FROZEN SALAD

Margaret Jarrett, Anderson, IN

8-oz. pkg. cream cheese, softened
1 cup sugar
1 pkg. frozen, cranberry orange relish
1 cup chopped nuts
15-oz. can crushed pineapple, drained
1 tsp. lemon juice
1 cup whipping cream

1. Cream together cream cheese and sugar. Add cranberry orange relish and fold in nuts. Add pineapple and lemon juice and mix well.
2. Beat whipping cream until stiff. Fold into salad mixture. Chill in refrigerator at least overnight. May be frozen before serving if desired.

Makes 10-12 servings

BLUEBERRY SALAD

Tommie Freeman, Carrollton, GA

2 3-oz. pkgs. blackberry gelatin
2 cups boiling water
15-oz. can blueberries
8-oz. can crushed pineapple
8-oz. pkg. cream cheese
½ cup sugar
1 cup sour cream
½ tsp. vanilla
1 cup chopped pecans

1. Dissolve gelatin in boiling water.
2. Drain blueberries and pineapple, reserving liquid. Add enough water to liquid to make 1½ cups. Stir liquid into gelatin mixture. Stir in blueberries and pineapple and pour into 9" x 13" casserole dish. Refrigerate until set.
3. Cream together cream cheese and sugar. Add sour cream and vanilla and mix well. Spread over salad. Sprinkle with chopped pecans and serve.

Makes 10-12 servings

RASPBERRY CROWN SALAD

Anita Falk, Mountain Lake, MN

3-oz. pkg. raspberry gelatin
2 cups boiling water
¾ cup cranberry juice
1 cup diced apples
¼ cup chopped celery
¼ cup chopped walnuts
3-oz. pkg. lemon gelatin
1 cup whipped topping
½ cup mayonnaise

1. Dissolve raspberry gelatin in 1 cup boiling water. Add cranberry juice and chill about 1 hour, until slightly thickened. Fold in apples, celery and walnuts. Spoon into 6-cup ring mold and chill until set, about 15 minutes.
2. Dissolve lemon gelatin in 1 cup boiling water. Chill until slightly thickened, about 45 minutes.
3. Combine whipped topping and mayonnaise and fold into lemon gelatin. Spoon onto raspberry gelatin. Chill until firm, at least 4 hours.
4. Unmold and serve.

Makes 8-10 servings

MOM'S CIDER SALAD

LuAnne S. Taylor, Canton, PA

3-oz. pkg. lemon gelatin
2 cups hot cider
2 Tbsp. lemon juice
1 cup chopped red apples
½ cup broken walnuts
½ cup sliced, pitted dates
1 Tbsp. grated orange rind (optional)
8 lettuce leaves

1. Dissolve gelatin in hot cider. Add lemon juice and chill until partially set.
2. Fold in apples, walnuts, dates and orange rind. Turn into 1-quart mold. Chill until firm.
3. Serve on lettuce leaves.

Makes 8 servings

GRAPE SALAD

Ann Harrison, Garland, TX

2 Tbsp. butter or *margarine*
2 Tbsp. flour
1 cup milk
1 large bag marshmallows
2 lbs. seedless green grapes
15-oz. can crushed pineapple, drained
1 cup chopped pecans

1. Melt butter in saucepan. Add flour and stir until bubbly. Add milk and heat over low temperature until mixture thickens, stirring frequently. Add marshmallows and continue heating, stirring constantly until marshmallows are melted.
2. Remove from heat and stir in grapes, pineapple and pecans.
3. Refrigerate several hours before serving.

Makes 10-12 servings

PINEAPPLE CUSTARD SALAD

Betty Caudle, Colorado Springs, CO

6-oz. pkg. lemon gelatin
2 cups boiling water
1½ cups cold water
20-oz. can crushed pineapple
4 bananas, diced
2 cups miniature marshmallows
¾ cup sugar
3 Tbsp. flour
2 eggs, beaten
1½ cups pineapple juice
3 Tbsp. butter
3-oz. pkg. cream cheese
1 cup whipped topping
¼ cup grated cheddar cheese

1. Dissolve gelatin in boiling water. Stir in cold water and let set until syrupy.
2. Drain pineapple, reserving juice.
3. Stir pineapple, bananas and marshmallows into partially set gelatin. Chill until firm.
4. Meanwhile, combine sugar, flour, eggs, pineapple juice and butter in top of double boiler. Cook until thickened, stirring occasionally. Cool.
5. Cream cream cheese with mixer. Combine cream cheese and whipped topping and fold into cooled custard mix. Spread over firm gelatin and sprinkle with grated cheese.

Makes 15-20 servings

When I was expecting our first child, we were enjoying a weekend visit from my parents and paternal grandmother from Iowa and my maternal grandmother from Pennsylvania. My mother-in-law suggested on the spur of the moment that we quilt a baby quilt while "we have all these quilting grandmas together." So we five women spent the next several days around the quilt anticipating the arrival of a new generation in our family. We sent the quilt to Texas where my husband's only living grandmother sewed the binding on, and I had a baby quilt stitched and bound with love by six women from three generations.

Karen Unternahrer, Shipshewana, IN

DUMP SALAD

Joyce Niemann, Fruitland Park, FL

8-oz. can crushed pineapple, well drained
3-oz. pkg. orange or lime gelatin
8-oz. carton cottage cheese
4-oz. carton whipped topping
6 lettuce leaves

1. Combine pineapple and dry gelatin and mix until gelatin has dissolved. Dump in cottage cheese and whipped topping and stir.
2. Refrigerate until serving time.
3. Serve on 6 individual plates on beds of lettuce.

Makes 6 servings

Each Tuesday I attend the meeting of the Bloomingdale Grange Quilters where we spend time quilting and enjoying a potluck lunch. Believe it or not, our dues are still only 10 cents a year.
Eleanor Larson, Glen Lyon, PA

LAZY DAY SALAD

Dorothy Shank, Sterling, IL

16-oz. can crushed pineapple, drained
16-oz. can fruit cocktail, drained
2 11-oz. cans mandarin oranges, drained
1 small pkg. instant vanilla pudding
8-oz. carton whipped topping
1 cup chopped pecans

1. Combine pineapple, fruit cocktail, oranges, dry pudding and whipped topping. Mix well and chill.
2. Sprinkle pecans over top and serve.

Makes 8-10 servings

ORANGE SALAD

Mildred Kennel, Atglen, PA

3-oz. pkg. orange gelatin
24-oz. carton cottage cheese
20-oz. can crushed pineapple or *fruit cocktail, drained*
11-oz. can mandarin oranges, drained
8-oz. carton whipped topping

1. Reserve 1 cup juice from pineapple and oranges. Bring to a boil and combine with orange gelatin. Chill until partially set.
2. Fold all remaining ingredients into partially set gelatin.
3. Refrigerate until firm and serve.

Makes 10-12 servings

Even though I am legally blind, I was able to piece a Lone Star wall hanging in Christmas colors last summer. I put masking tape on my sewing machine to indicate where the fabric should be as I stitched it.

Mary Elizabeth Bartlet, Schenectady, NY

ORANGE GELATIN SALAD

Vivian Angstadt, Mertztown, PA

6-oz. pkg. orange gelatin
½ cup sugar
½ cup boiling water
2 cups whipped topping
8-oz. pkg. cream cheese
11-oz. can mandarin oranges

1. Dissolve gelatin and sugar in boiling water. Let cool until starting to set.
2. Beat together whipped topping and cream cheese. Stir until smooth.
3. When gelatin has slightly set, fold in oranges with their juice. Fold in whipped topping mixture.
4. Refrigerate overnight before serving.

Makes 10 servings

GINGERALE SALAD

Sarah S. King, Gordonville, PA

Layer 1
2 Tbsp. unflavored gelatin
2½ Tbsp. cold water
1 cup boiling water
¾ cup sugar
2 Tbsp. lemon juice
2 cups gingerale
8-oz. can crushed pineapple
1 cup diced apples

Layer 2
2 Tbsp. flour
½ cup sugar
2 eggs, beaten
1½ Tbsp. butter
1 cup pineapple juice
8-oz. container whipped topping
1 cup chopped nuts (optional)

1. To prepare first layer dissolve gelatin in cold water. Add boiling water and sugar and stir until dissolved. Add lemon juice and gingerale. Chill until partially set.
2. Drain pineapple and reserve juice. Fold pineapple and apples into gelatin. Pour into pan or mold and chill until set.
3. To prepare second layer combine flour and sugar in a saucepan. Add eggs, butter and 1 cup pineapple juice (add water to make 1 cup if necessary). Heat through, stirring constantly. Cool completely.
4. Fold in whipped topping. Spoon over first layer and sprinkle with nuts if desired. Serve.

Makes 12-15 servings

M y grandmother was a quilter and I have many memories of sitting beside her, listening and watching as she sewed her quilts. We used these quilts on our beds, as ground cover at picnics, to turn chairs into rainy day caves and to make tents out of clothesline. Today they are my heirlooms, but they certainly were not handled with white gloves.

Grace K. Bruce, Alguquerque, NM

INDEX